Aaron Adams

804 N Delaware

Indianapolis, IN 46204

aaron@alpinecs.com

www.alpinecapitalsolutions.com

Tips Tricks Foreclosures and Flips
Of a Millionaire Real Estate Investor

By Aaron Adams

Table of Contents

4

Who Am I?

Fourteen years ago I was teaching U.S. History and Spanish in a large high school. I made less than $40,000/year and had over $200,000 in debt. I wasn't financially destitute, and I actually had excellent credit. I was living the typical American Dream of a mortgage, a car payment, credit card bills, and a 9-5 (well actually 7-3 for teachers ☺) job. One Friday night I saw an infomercial that changed my life.

My wife was out of town, and I was home alone on the couch watching TV. As I channel surfed,

I stopped on an infomercial about real estate investing. My interest peaked, I jumped on the internet and purchased a used version of this same investing program for $20 on eBay. The course arrived a few days later and I began to read.

Ironically enough, at this same time, I was also working on completing an MBA at California Polytechnic Institute in Pomona California. I had been taking MBA classes for almost a year when I purchased the real estate investing book. I was mildly irritated none of my professors had taught me any of the techniques I was learning in this book. As I look back, I now know it was because my professors themselves were living the 'American Dream' as I was, and hadn't found a way to make more money, much less in real estate!

After finishing the book, I had a ton of questions. But being a risk taker at heart, I decided to plunge in and buy an investment property. I found a duplex in Hemet, California that I could buy for $100,000. It needed about $10,000 in work, but would generate $750 a month per side. After realizing I could live in one side and pay my mortgage from the rent on the other side, I put my three bedroom house on the market to sell and jumped in with both feet!

Through all my years of college I was fortunate to have the opportunity to work full time and pay for my tuition, books, and fees without having to borrow any student loan money. I ended up taking out a student loan to pay for the $10,000 repairs the duplex needed. Between borrowing the 3% down I needed for the mortgage, borrowing the money I needed for closing costs, and borrowing the money I needed for the rehab on the duplex, I basically borrowed 100% of the purchase and rehab costs I needed to own this duplex. I hadn't spent ONE PENNY of my own money to buy this property!

A few short months later, I was able to sell my duplex for $175,000! After the closing, I sat there looking at the thousands and thousands of dollars I had just earned, and thought how little time I had spent "earning" that money. It was at this moment a fire began to burn inside me and still burns today. Almost 2000 properties later, and I have purchased single family homes, duplexes, apartment complexes, and trailer parks. I have also been involved in hard money lending, private equity partnerships, new construction, and almost every type of business transaction existing for real estate.

The most important lesson I have learned is this: real estate is BEST learned from one person

This is just one example of the many techniques I teach investors at my Bus Tours I give all over the country www.alpinecs.com

to another –face to face, with question and answer.

My purpose of this book is NOT to teach you everything you need to know about real estate. I found it impossible to learn what to do with question and answer. I had mentors and experienced investors who taught me the pros and cons of each strategy, who helped me pick an individualized strategy for where I was living and the real estate climate that existed in early 2000. What I really hope to accomplish is to give you some ideas and proven techniques I have used over and over again to make money, AND to paint a picture of ways you can begin making money from real estate investing in just a short amount of time.

For those of you who already have some real estate investing experience, there may be some new ideas you haven't thought of before OR some new ways to use old ideas with which you are—already familiar. None of these ideas are 100% mine, but the experiences are and they are backed by the hundreds and hundreds of properties I have purchased over the years. ENJOY the tips and tricks, and I look forward to meeting you face to face at one of our events down the road.

Chapter One – USING PUBLIC RECORDS TO

FIND HOME RUN DEALS

A couple of years ago, I went down to our city offices and pulled up the tax records on an apartment complex. Tax records are public records and anyone has access to them. In fact, most realtors have access to tax records online and they are easy to search. I noticed the mailing address for this apartment complex was different than the address of the apartment complex itself. This made sense to me because I assumed the apartment complex owner was NOT living at his own property. I also figured the owner would NOT want his tax bills mailed TO the apartment complex because he wanted to get them at his OWN house.

Next, I took a look at how long the investor had owned the apartment complex. In this case, he and his wife had owned it for over 35 years! This was very interesting to me because I decided these owners may be interested in selling the property if someone offered them the right amount. I knew that often times, investors who own multi-family properties think the properties need to be in pristine condition or completely full if they are going to be able to sell them. I was hoping these owners had interest to sell but just needed someone to drop an offer right into their lap.

After deciding to write an offer on this property, I had to figure out how much to offer the owner. If I offered too much, I would leave money on the table; offering too low would guarantee the owner would throw my offer in the garbage. This particular property was in a highly distressed condition. I knew it would need a couple hundred thousand dollars in work to get it back up to great shape. I also knew that if the owner listed the property on the market, they would probably be able to get $75-$100K for it. Gambling that, one, the property was in bad shape, and, two, the owner would think it was worth less money, I sent them a letter:

Dear investor,

My name is Aaron Adams. I am an investor who is very interested in buying your property located at 1234 Main Street, Indianapolis, IN. I would be willing to pay you $35,000 all cash two days after your acceptance of my offer. I will pay you all cash and will take the property AS-IS. The only thing I require is clean title and for property taxes to be paid current. My number is (xxx-xxx-xxxx) Please call me at your earliest convenience if this is something you are interested in pursuing.

14

The letter went out on a Monday. By Tuesday it was delivered, and on Wednesday I received a phone call. One week later, the owner got his check, and I got an apartment complex for $35,000. However, in that week before closing, I had a tough dilemma to solve: I was tempted to call several investors I knew and offer them the chance to buy the property for $50,000-$75,000. When the seller and I signed the Purchase Agreement, I gave him $1000 earnest money. But, imagine I had flipped this deal to another investor for $75,000! I would have made $40,000 just for being willing to go to the city offices and search the tax records and to commit $1000 of my money.

This is a perfect example of how to generate tens of thousands of dollars by being proactive. Investors who think "in the box" wait for a deal to come up on the market.

But millionaires know the best deals are waiting to be
found by proactive, positive, and polite inquiries.

Key Points to Remember

- Public Tax Records can reveal a lot about a property
- Search records to find addresses that are different from the physical address and the mailing address
- Search records to find owners who have owned properties for a long time
- Politely and proactively reach out to these owners and offer them a specific amount for their property
- Consider going by the investors' home and leaving a letter with a hand written note so your letter isn't viewed as junk mail
- Develop a network of investors who you can flip deals to for a quick profit

Chapter Two – USING HAND DELIVERED

LETTERS TO GET DEALS

In 2002 I found a website that charged a small monthly fee to give information on properties in foreclosure. This website tracked lenders who filed foreclosure proceedings against homeowners more than 60 days behind on their mortgage payments. I quickly learned many investors like myself would send a letter of interest to homeowners who were in pre-foreclosure stage in order to see if a deal could be worked out to buy the home BEFORE the property was foreclosed by the bank and sold at auction.

I wracked my brain to think of a way to distinguish MY letters from the ones other investors sent to homeowners in pre-foreclosure. I decided the best method would be to attempt a personal contact to the homeowners. If I could connect with them, I could convince them to work with me

in selling their home.

> **3 Stages of Foreclosure**
>
> - **Pre-Foreclosure**: **Owner is behind on his mortgage payment**
> - **Foreclosure**: **Property is auctioned off at public auction**
> - **REO**: **Property is not sold at auction, goes back to the bank (Real Estate Owned) and is usually listed with an REO broker**

In today's real estate market, most homeowners who are in pre-foreclosure stage are upside down on their homes. This means they owe MORE for their mortgage than what their home is worth. Back in 2002 however, the market was going up in value at a record pace in California. There were some areas of Riverside County where I lived, where the values were increasing 4-6% in value PER MONTH. I knew I just had to get a deal under contract, and the rapid appreciation in the market would handle the rest for me.

Searching the foreclosure website I paid a subscription to, I found a home near me where the homeowner only owed $60,000 to the bank. They were two months behind to the bank, and there was a good chance they would lose the home in a couple more months. I drove by the home and could tell, just from the exterior of the home, and the neighborhood, the house was worth over $100,000.

The next day I put together a letter similar to the one I outlined in Chapter 1. But instead of mailing the letter, I took it to the house. When I knocked on the door, a 6'2", 300 lb+ Hispanic man answered the door. He looked mean and NOT happy to see me. Drawing on my two years spent in Venezuela as a missionary, I cleared my throat and said, "Hello, I am sorry to bother you… my name is Aaron

Adams and I wanted to come by and offer you $60,000 cash for this house." Somewhat surprised, he stared at me for a good ten seconds and said (in broken English), "You are not selling nothing?" I immediately switched to Spanish and repeated my offer. Once he heard my Spanish, within five minutes I was invited into the house, seated, drinking a soda, and outlining my offer.

One of the first questions I was dying to ask was why they hadn't just thrown the house on the market for $70K and listed it for a quick sale. They explained that after losing their jobs, they believed they were going to get caught up on the mortgage. Furthermore, by the time they starting going through all the mail they had received from other investors like me, they were so confused. Thinking they were going to be scammed, they decided to let the bank auction the property. This decision was reinforced by some friends from their church who had lost a home to foreclosure and had actually been sent a check AFTER the auction because the home had sold for MORE than they owed for the payoff + penalties + fees. They figured it would be the least complicated way to get out of the whole situation.

Over the next week, I met with this family no less than ten times. Although they agreed to sell me the house for $65,000, they also hit me up for money to rent a U-Haul, to hire someone to help them load up the truck, and even asked me to give them money for first and last month's rent for their new apartment they were going to rent! At first I was mildly irritated, but quickly reminded myself the big picture was most important and after spending $15K on the house, I was going to be able to sell it for $120,000 easily.

By developing a personal relationship with the homeowner, a bad situation was fixed, their credit was saved, the homeowners walked away from the deal with a little cash in their pocket, and I ended up with a house that cleared me a little over $25,000 when all was said and done. I am sure my competitors who sent mailers wondered why their fancy postcards, letters, and graphics didn't result in a deal. They very well may have been willing to work a deal out face to face, but I was the only one who showed up on their doorstep, took the time to find out how I could help THEM and closed the deal. Over the years, I have ALWAYS found that my BEST deals have come from face to face encounters with motivated sellers.

Key Points to Remember

- Personal contact with a motivated seller is the BEST way to get a deal
- Focus on finding out what the seller NEEDS to get out of the deal
- Sincerely try to help them find a way out of their problems with the least amount of damage
- Be clear with the seller about what YOU will be getting from the transaction
- Keep the big picture in mind throughout the whole process
- Always remember that if you are willing to do a little bit more than your competitor in the short term it will pay off HUGE in the long run

Chapter Three – USING YARD SIGNS TO FIND

MOTIVATED SELLERS

Never underestimate the power of marketing. TV, radio, billboards, and internet are all excellent ways to find sellers and deals, tenants for your houses, and buyers who want properties in which to live or invest. However, TV, radio, billboards, and internet can be expensive.

One of the first multifamily properties I purchased was a 7-plex. It consisted of ½ a city block with 2 duplexes, and 3 small houses all on 3 lots. (There is no way a property like this would get approved by zoning today, but since all of these properties were built pre-1950, zoning laws were more lax back then!) After completing extensive rehab on all the properties, I quickly needed to find tenants as I had a

mortgage to pay every month!

Prior to this property, I had only owned one other

multifamily

property – a

duplex that was

easy to keep

rented. This

was the first

time I would

had to find

tenants on my

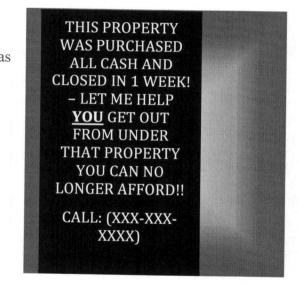

own. I began by running ads in the local newspaper and

the free circular known as the *Penny Saver*. As an

afterthought, I also put up "For Rent" signs I had purchased

at Home Depot. Much to my surprise, the majority of my

calls started coming in from the signs I had placed at the property. I quickly rented out all seven units and forgot about those signs. However, I continued to get four to five calls a week due to the "For Rent" sign still at the property. I didn't have any other property for rent, but I started to think there HAD to be a use for those leads. I called a couple of property management companies to see if they wanted to buy my leads for rentals, but they weren't really interested since they had yard signs of their own that generated leads. After thinking about it for a while, it occurred to me that maybe I could buy blank signs and use them to find motivated sellers looking to get rid of their properties. I went back to Home Depot and created the following sign:

While I didn't get three to five calls a week, I DID start to get one or two calls every few weeks with someone who had seen the sign and was interested. To my amazement, from just that one sign, I ended up finding an investor who owned multiple properties in town and from whom, over the next few years, I was able to buy FIVE investment properties. Since that time, I have NEVER neglected the chance to market my deals in any way, shape, or form!

Everyone has seen signs on corners at intersections or stapled up on telephone poles that say some variation of "WE BUY HOUSES – CASH." I have found that by putting up a sign in a neighborhood where I have already purchased a property, I get multiple additional benefits.

First, I have established the ability to market in an area where I want to buy the same neighborhood where other potentially motivated sellers live, work, and drive every day. Second, I describe the way I buy deals, which acknowledges I understand the seller is distressed and/or motivated. Finally, if this person notices the sign, I am hopeful he noticed I came in and spent money on a distressed property. I have found this conveys my financial wherewithal, and confirms to them MY ability to come through and buy their property.

As I have scaled up my operations, I have used everything from Craigslist to television commercials to market our business. But I still find that good old fashion yard signs

---

Key Points to Remember

- You can skimp on some things but NEVER skimp too much on marketing
- Utilize all avenues of marketing that you can afford
- Try to respond to inquiries from your ads within MINUTES of their call
- Handwritten yard signs can sometimes be more effective than printed signs because they seem less intimidating and more personal
- DO NOT be misleading in your ads – it starts the relationship on the WRONG foot

are an effective and cheap way to get the word out and get

phone calls rolling in.

Chapter Four – FINDING WHERE ALL THE REAL INVESTORS HANG OUT (IT'S NOT AT REAL ESTATE INVESTING CLUBS!!)

In November of 2004 I attended my first foreclosure auction with a friend of my father's. Rick worked for a law firm in town and had bought almost a hundred properties at auction, so he was very experienced and, MORE IMPORTANTLY, was known to the major investors who purchased there every month.

In fascination, I watched as Rick analyzed the starting bid prices for bank owned properties for sale. They were all laid out on several dry erase boards and organized by starting bid amount. This amount correlated to a number. In order to get the address, Rick consulted a spreadsheet he had printed off from the county Sheriff's department which listed the sale numbers, the addresses, and how much the home owner owed the bank (the judgment).

Rick said to me, "Since this is your first auction, and you only brought $20,000 in cashier's checks, we won't look at anything with a starting bid over $19,500 because you can only bid up to what you have on deposit." We then identified five properties all with starting bid prices under $19,500.

As we left the county building, I asked Rick if each of the houses had a lockbox so we could get in and check them out. He smiled and said, "Aaron, this is the foreclosure auction. The best we can do is look in the window of the house – and if they are occupied, we can't even do that!" I then asked, "How long do we have to check these houses out?" To which he replied, "3 hours. We have to be back downtown with our bids submitted and ready for the auction to start by 3:30pm, so we will need to hustle in order to see all five!"

For the next two hours, Rick and I would quickly drive to a house, get out of the car, walk around the house, peek in the windows, and determine if it was a good deal for the starting sale price. One house in particular caught my eye. The starting bid price was only $11,500, and when we peeked in the windows, it looked like it only needed a few thousand dollars in rehab. I turned to Rick and gushed, "This one is amazing! Home run! I bet everyone at the auction will be bidding on it. Do you think we will be able to get it for less than $20,000?"

Rick laughed and replied, "Aaron, this is why so many investors come to the auction and fail. This house isn't worth $20,000 – in fact it's priced too high at $11,500. I wouldn't pay a penny over $8000 for it." Looking at the house again, and then looking back at Rick I was completely skeptical. Rick explained further, "One street east of here, one of the biggest gangs in the city operates. Not much happens without their permission. If you bought this house and started fixing it up without their "blessing", you would probably find that every time you are trying to fix it up, things get stolen and it gets broken into. And every time a tenant moves in they aren't happy with, they will somehow decide not to complete their lease and move out on you."

The rest of the time, Rick went on in great detail about the pros and cons of buying houses at auction. We went back downtown and watched the same five or six investors buy 90% of the inventory. When asked about it, Rick smiled and said, "Once you figure out how to navigate the pitfalls and have a system to buy, it's one of the easiest ways to consistently get "A+" deals every month!

In that instant, I made a promise to myself I was going to figure out how to buy at auction. I would build my own system to quickly evaluate starting bids and addresses, develop intimate street-by-street knowledge of neighborhoods, and learn to ballpark construction amounts just from looking at the outside of the house. Since November of 2004, I have purchased HUNDREDS and HUNDREDS of properties at foreclosure auctions. I have also learned how to by properties at tax auctions and have successfully incorporated that methods to acquire "A+" deals. I have been to auctions in California, Texas, and Indiana, and the one common denominator with every single one is that the same faces and companies appear over and over again, proving once you figure out a good system,

it's not difficult to buy at the auction. I see people come
and go every month. It's usually because they overestimate
the rent, or overestimate the after repair value or
underestimate the amount of rehab. At my two day bus
tours in Indianapolis, we teach how to buy at foreclosure
auctions all over the country. I have helped investors go
back to their home state, avoid the traps, and buy "A+"
deals of their own!

Chapter Five – USING PROPERTY

MANAGEMENT COMPANIES TO FIND DEALS

About a year ago, we got a call at our property management offices in Indianapolis from an attorney. He indicated he was representing the estate from one of our recently deceased investors. The two homes the investor owned had been passed to his two children, and they wanted to sell the properties.

I looked up the performance of Cliff's two houses. Cliff purchased them eighteen months before for $62,000 each. They rented for $688/month and $725/month. We collected rent and sent it to him faithfully for 17 out of the 18 months. The homes had been built in 1993, and although they were in a working class area, they would stay rented easily and for a long time.

I called the attorney back and told him Cliff's adult children had inherited two excellent cash flow properties. I told him it would be a mistake to sell them because the value had only gone up a few thousand dollars in the eighteen months he owned them, and Cliff's original strategy was to hold them five to ten years, giving them time for solid appreciation, excellent cash flow returns, AND the chance for monthly rent to increase. After hearing my reasoning, the attorney agreed and said he would try to convince Cliff's kids to keep the houses as there was no mortgage to be paid on them.

I didn't hear from Cliff's attorney for a few months, but got an email from him later. Cliff's children had originally been willing to keep the two houses, but unfortunately had been fighting over other aspects of the estate and decided to sell both properties as quickly as possible.

Benefits of owning cash flow properties

- 10%+ returns on your money
- Security of owning property
- Steady income
- Tax write offs
- High amount of control
- Appreciation potential

Since both were still rented, it would take a while to sell the home to a homeowner because both leases would need terminated and the properties rehabbed. I also mentioned the best choice was to sell to another investor like Cliff who had all cash and wanted to own the houses for the same reasons as Cliff.

After the attorney discussed this in detail, they were willing to take $54,000 for each house if I could find a buyer quickly to get them out of the deal. There was a very good chance we could find a buyer since we managed another fifty plus homes just in that same neighborhood. That being said, a letter was sent out to THOSE investors giving them first dibs on buying the property and for less than any previously purchased homes.

The email went out on a Thursday, and by Friday afternoon, I had four responses from investors ready and willing to buy. SHOCKED how strong the interest was, I mentioned to my staff we needed to be marketing MORE investment properties directly to our current landlords as very few take the initiative to write US and ask for deals. Once we put an "A+" deal in front of them, they tended to jump at it quickly.

After the properties closed, Cliff's attorney commented to me that our network of investors all over the country were lucky to be part of our management group. He said, "As an estate attorney, I see all sorts of good and bad real estate investments that people leave their heirs, I can tell you Cliff made an excellent decision to invest with you while he was living and the benefits of your system carried over to his children AFTER his death. You are to be congratulated for such an excellent, integrated investing option!" I smiled and replied, "I couldn't agree more! We have spent twelve years developing and honing our purchasing, rehabbing, renting, managing, and selling program. Now that we have hundreds of properties under management for investors all over the world, we are truly *reaping what we sowed*"!

Key Points to Remember

- Get to know the large and small property management companies that manage properties where you invest
- Find out what their investors consider an "A+" deal
- Offer the property management company owner a commission if they will market your deals to investors who could be looking and for whom they manage properties
- Offer to buy deals they manage if they fall in your "A+" range

Chapter Six – CREATIVELY SELLING PROPERTIES TO OTHER INVESTORS

One of the best ways to sell properties is to other investors. I have one client who regularly buys properties from me. It's nice because I have created demand for my houses that surpasses my ability to keep up with supply. The first four years I was buying and selling properties, my primary focus was ~~on~~ selling to homeowners after listing my properties on MLS. This makes sense to all beginning investors because many of us own homes and that is how we found OUR home.

The problem with using MLS sales as the primary method to move deals is that you are completely subject to the whims of the marketplace. Supply and demand are constantly changing in every state, city, and neighborhood. Average days on the market in a given neighborhood can fluctuate wildly from one month to the next.

At one point in 2003, I had almost every penny of investment capital (almost $1MM) invested into homes on MLS. This amounted to nine properties. Some of my closings were held up. Some cancelled and I had to quickly resell them, but it got to the point that summer where all of the money was in properties with buyers trying to close them, and I was completely cash poor.

> *"A balanced real estate portfolio should have 50% being long term cash flow properties, 25% MLS flips, 20% investor flips and 5% wholesaling. This will ensure enough cash flow, tax benefits and*

I remember distinctly calling title and escrow companies every day to check the status of my closings. The end of

July came and went, and I was forced to use my credit cards to pay my bills. As August crept along, and none of the properties closed, I began losing sleep as I realized if I couldn't get these deals closed by the end of September, I could easily be forced into bankruptcy by my creditors!! Imagine my anxiety, knowing that with those 9 deals, I was waiting on several hundred thousand dollars in just PROFIT.

Fortune finally turned my way and properties started closing. I promised myself to never be so dependent again on one source of property sales. Going forward, I would buy more cash flow properties so I could have rent money coming in every month to pay bills. I also felt it was important to wholesale some deals pre-rehab to generate quick cash flow. Finally, that I would sell a greater percentage of my properties to investors who had cash to buy and close quickly. Since that time, I have never sold more than 25% of my properties on MLS.

As I switched my focus from MLS deals to investor deals, I struggled initially to find a good outlet of investors looking for cash flow properties I could sell and then manage for them after closing. Quickly I learned one of the best ways to find investors is to be around a group of realtors who occasionally have clients who want to buy a rental.

Prior to this time, I had completed my Real Estate Broker's license in the state of California. I held it independently because I didn't think there was really any good reason for me to join another brokerage. However, as I looked to scale up my sales to investors, I decided that by joining the biggest brokerage in town and hanging my shingle with them, I would have a whole bunch of real estate agents I could market my investment properties to and that they could take to their clients as "pocket listings."

This turned out to be extremely successful. Within months, all the realtors in the firm were checking with me ANY time they had a client express an interest in multi-family properties or rental houses. They all knew what a great job I did on my rehabs and that in order to ensure the properties success, I was willing to manage the property for their client after closing. They loved this because it was like a built-in warranty in quality of work done to the property and quality of tenants placed there.

Chris is a friend of mine and has been a contractor for many years. He has flipped many properties to investors over the years. Chris had a brilliant idea. He utilized his contractor skills as a way to find investors who wanted deals.

Chris started a construction company specializing in "punch list" rehab work. "Punch list" rehab work is the final list of items needing completion before a homeowner can buy a home, get their loan, and move in. Punch lists are usually generated by the buyers as a result of home inspections done on the property or appraisals the bank has ordered. They can include items as simple as painting the mailbox, or be as complicated as replacing breakers in the electrical panel.

Realtors love using Chris and his company because his crew will do every little item on the punch list with great pricing. Chris now has a huge number of realtors who use his company's construction services, and he parlays those relationships into opportunities to sell his cash flow properties. In the same way that I had a group of realtors who would market my deals to their clients who wanted to buy rentals, Chris has a group of realtors he can send his properties who will offer them to investors they know!

Key Points to Remember

- Never be too dependent on one source of sales for your properties
- Look to get into the real estate industry indirectly so you can build trust with people who know investors looking for deals
- If you want to sell to investors, consider getting into property management because it will give them more confidence in the quality of your product

Chapter Seven – FINDING MOTIVATED

BUYERS

For years I have been traveling the world, teaching investors the techniques and tricks I have developed to make millions in real estate. As a former high school teacher, there is nothing more satisfying for me than spending two or three days with a group of investors, educating them on real estate, then watching them go back to their respective homes and change their lives.

There   is an old saying:

> *"If you give a man a fish you will feed him for that day. Teach him to fish and you will feed him for a lifetime"*

> *"If you teach a man to fish you feed him*
> *for a lifetime but let him take the fish*
> *home you caught that day so he has*
> *something to eat that night!!"*
> *Aaron Adams*

I love this quotation except I would like to rewrite the quote:

We have found investors come to our seminars ready to take action. We sell many properties directly to investors AT our seminars in addition to helping them find a supply of their own cash flow properties from their hometown. Many investors simply decide it's easier to outsource ALL of their cash flow properties with us because we have such a large system in place; they would rather focus on flipping deals than taking maintenance calls from their tenants.

A couple of years ago, I received a call from an investor who told me he was completing a 1031 exchange, and he needed five cash flow properties within 48 hours. I LOVED this call because at that time, I had about twenty properties available to sell and was happy to get him the five he needed. (A 1031 exchange is a way to defer paying taxes from profit you make from selling another property).

Realizing there are investors all over the country (and actually all over the WORLD)who needed good properties, in a stable market, with built in property management services, was probably the biggest single motivator pushing me to seek ways to reach a worldwide audience for our product. Some people call this "turnkey" investing.

I began working with two different companies that would have seminars and invite me to teach on my experiences in real estate, and specifically talk about the cash flow property MACHINE we had built in Indianapolis. As I explained to them the 150+ people who worked with our company, and told of the hundreds of properties we manage as well as the thousands of hours of experience our staff collectively had, we were able to sell hundreds of properties to people all over the world.

To meet people every month who have had poor experiences investing on their own or in the stock market and be able to offer them a product that easily makes them 10% or more per year on their money is fantastic! We have literally had seminars where investors buy every single deal we bring PLUS give us deposits for the next round of properties we are buying at auction.

I have a friend who goes to conventions that attract self-directed IRA clients from all over the county (A self-directed IRA allows one to invest his retirement money into almost anything… -stocks, bonds, and, yes, real estate). The difference is, the investor (YOU) controls what, when, and where to buy.

He then offers and sells his cash flow properties at these events. He walks into a room full of "hungry" investors

Key Points to Remember

- Always try to keep a supply of a few more properties than you think you need – you NEVER know when someone will call looking for properties to buy from you
- Be creative and find buyers who already know they want deals where you invest
- Make sure you understand what your future client will think is an "A+" deal for both wholesale AND turnkey deals

looking for good deals and good properties and walks out

with a stack of purchase agreements.

Chapter Eight – SELLING TO TENANTS –

WORKING BACKWARDS TO FIND A BUYER

Heather had been a renter for many years. She had great credit, always had a job, but wasn't great at saving her money. She always lived within her means, but never had much extra cash at the end of the month.

Heather mistakenly thought she needed "a lot" of down payment money to buy a home. She thought she would have to save up $10k-20K to purchase a home. On top of that, Heather was a worried about hidden costs of home ownership. She knew there wouldn't be a maintenance line to call, and she would be responsible for cutting the grass, unclogging the toilets, paying the taxes, and trimming the trees.

I purchased a home at foreclosure auction in a quiet, middle class neighborhood close to downtown Indianapolis: quiet streets, parks and mostly homeowners needing less than $10,000 in cosmetic rehab (carpet, paint, fixtures). I picked it up at auction for $65,000 and knew after rehab, it would easily appraise for $110,000.

After the auction, I knew what a great house this was and I thought to list the house on MLS to sell. My office manager knew a renter interested in buying, and Heather was the FIRST person I approached.

Heather met with me the next week to discuss purchasing the home. She had already driven by the house and was very interested in what I had to say.

When we sat down in my office, I said to Heather, "What would you say if I told you I could help you own a home nicer than the apartment you rent right now and for less a month than what you pay in rent." She replied, "I'm all ears." I explained that if she could find a way to save/borrow $5000, I could let her pick EVERYTHING about the house. The paint colors, the flooring, even the type of countertops and fixtures she wanted. I also pointed out that she was currently paying $925/month for her apartment and based on current interest rates, her mortgage, taxes, AND insurance wouldn't be more than $740/month.

Heather was stunned and almost in tears. She had always dreamed of owning a home, but figured she wouldn't like anything she could afford, and wasn't confident with any aspect of the process. When I explained we would walk her through every step of the way, and that if she ever needed it, she could draw on my maintenance guys and contractors for expert guidance, she was THRILLED!

Over the next few months Heather and the contractor worked on every aspect of the rehab. She epitomized "pride of ownership" as she worked tirelessly to create the perfect home. A few weeks after she moved in, she proudly showed off everything she had incorporated into her home. Today, I see her on Facebook and have noticed she entertains regularly at her house. It has become a focal point for her and her friends to meet up and be together.

The coolest part is this was truly a Win/Win for both of us.

I was able to make $10,000 net profit on the deal and

Heather couldn't have cared less. She figured it was worth

every penny considering what we were able to help her do.

Key Points to Remember

- Many people are still renters because they don't REALIZE they could be homeowners
- You could work closely with a property management company to identify great tenants that you could walk through the process of buying a home
- You could also go out and buy a home in the area that they want to live, rehab it to their specs and then sell it back to them for a pre-determined profit amount

Chapter Nine – SELLING TO TENANTS – BE

THE BANK

The highest amount of profit I ever made was as a trailer park owner. Trailer parks are CASH COWS! Not only did I collect the space rent every month, but I made money off the vending machines and also owned most of the trailers in the park that I sold to the tenants and let them pay me on contract.

I met Maria and her two year old son in 2003. I had owned the park for a little while and had a small 12x50' single wide trailer just rehabbed. I purchased it dirt cheap for $4000 and spent another

$3000 fixing it up ($3000 goes a LONG way in a trailer that's only 600 square feet!)

Maria originally called me asking if I was planning on renting any of the trailers. She had just found work at one restaurant in town and was earning $500-700/week. I explained we didn't rent ANY of the trailers in the park. I then explained we had a 12x50' single wide for sale and, if she could come up with the $3000 down payment, I would finance the other $7000 for her (be the bank). Maria replied she had bad credit. I explained I didn't pull credit at all, and if she could prove her employment and come up with $3000, she could move in the next day if she wanted.

Maria showed up that same day to check out the mobile home. It was in B+/A- condition and really wouldn't need any work for a long time. She asked me how much the payment would be. I said the $7000 she still owed could be paid over the next five years for just $159/month. I also told her the space rent would be another $250. She would still have to pay electric and gas, (approx. $100-150/mo.) but for $409, it would be all hers and absolutely affordable compared to the amount of money she was making a month. Maria was ecstatic, and after she had me explain it all over again to her brother over the phone, he loaned her the $3000 she needed to move in.

For the next four years, I received a check from Maria exactly on the first of the month. She took fantastic care of her little home and focused on working hard and raising her son. I found out a of couple years after she moved in that the father of her child was in a gang in LA. She had fled him and the gang lifestyle hoping for a better life for her son. I was so moved by her efforts, that six months before she had the mobile home paid off, I signed off on the title and mailed it to her. In it, I included a post-it note that said, "Good things come to those who embrace positive change! Congrats on being a free and clear homeowner."

I'll never forget Maria or the power of financing properties for tenants.

> ### Key Points to Remember
>
> - *Financing a property instead of renting it has a ton of benefits*
>   - *Eliminate property management headaches*
>   - *Eliminate variability of expenses*
>   - *Get max value for the asset*
>   - *Get higher interest rate*
>   - *Get down payment money*
> - *I have a friend who sources people to move into his homes he wants to finance by working with a mortgage broker to find people the almost but not quite qualified for a mortgage*

Chapter Ten – HOW TO GET $$ TO INVEST WHEN YOU ARE BROKE

I taught high school for three years while I was working on an MBA and flipping my first couple of deals. In addition to teaching High School, I coached girl's volleyball, boy's golf, and boy's soccer. Every day the coaches met in the athletic director's office and ate lunch together.

One of the recurring topics of conversation was the properties I was flipping. The other coaches (teachers) were VERY interested in what I paid for properties, how the rehab was going, when I listed them on the market, how much they sold for and, of course, how much profit I was making. Over these three years, they were converted from outright skeptical (*there's no way this market can last*), to begrudging approval (*nice, very nice... make sure you save it all*), to outright support (*what you are doing with these properties is amazing! When are you quitting teaching?!*). I personally enjoyed the daily banter and conversation. It forced me to be clear about my plans and defend them constantly.

One teacher by the name of Dick never said much at the daily lunches. He had been a health teacher in the same school system for 35 years. He was ready to retire, and, because he had a PhD, his pay scale would ensure he made over $8000/month for the rest of his life. The other coaches told me privately that Dick had a VERY interesting house/property. He had essentially converted a half acre parcel into his own personal museum of stuff he had collected over the years. I wouldn't say he was a "hoarder", but he had a ton of cool and different things spread out over his property. He was, however, VERY frugal with his money and NEVER spent the whole paycheck he received each month. In fact, I would be surprised if he even spent a third of it.

About a year into my flipping career, Dick pulled me aside one day and told me he wanted to meet with me about doing some investing together. I had no idea what that meant because Dick was a man of very few words. I said, "Well, I have a few deals I have kept my eye on but haven't been able to purchase because I am waiting for funds from a couple of properties that need to close." Dick then said, "Well how much can you put to work?" I was stumped because I didn't want to ask for too little and have him agree, but I was afraid if I asked for too much, he would think I was overreaching and be bugged.

I figured there was NO way he would want to invest more than $25-30K so I said, "Well, Dick, I could sure use

$40,000 right now to invest." Dick looked at me, scratched his head and replied, "That's really disappointing, because I have $250,000 cash in a savings account I have been hoping to put to work with you." I about fell off my chair and onto the floor! I never expected a high school teacher would want to roll the dice on a quarter million dollars!

After stammering out a reply, I assured Dick could keep all the money working and asked him how he wanted me to secure his money. He looked at me, stuck his hand out and said, "I want you to come to my house the first of the month, bring me a check for 1% simple interest ($2500), look me in the eye, and tell me you aren't stealing from me." I laughed and then said, "You know what, Dick? Either you are an excellent judge of character or really stupid, because I KNOW I would work at McDonalds before I would ever default on your retirement money or use it for ANYTHING other than real estate investments."

For the next three years until I moved to Indianapolis, I would head over to Dick's on the first of the month with a check for $2500. It was a fantastic partnership because in that time, I easily made over $750,000 off of his money.

Key Points to Remember

- You NEVER know who has money. Many will keep it a secret because they haven't had a good reason to let you know
- Never sell a partnership – sell deals
- Always make sure your investor partners can make a double digit return
- Treat the partnership as if there is 100% trust but document everything you do as if you are getting audited

Chapter Eleven – BUYING PROPERTIES IN THE US AT FORECLOSURE AUCTIONS

Over the past ten years I have purchased THOUSANDS of homes directly from foreclosure auctions. It remains one of my most reliable ways to source deeply discounted properties.

You ONLY make money in real estate when you buy cheaply. I am able to regularly buy properties at auctions for ten cents on the dollar. While I have been able to purchase some "grand-slam home run" deals, I have also bought horrible deals. Some of the risks of buying at U.S. foreclosure auctions include the following:

- You usually only have a few HOURS to figure out which properties you are going to bid on
- You could be purchasing a second mortgage which is worthless in terms of ownership
- Your property could have Internal Revenue Service liens placed on it
- You can't get into the property to inspect it (unless someone has kicked the door in!) so you have little to no idea of the interior condition
- You don't have guaranteed clear title
- You could have demolition orders or health and hospital liens from the local city or municipality

As you can see with any reward there are always risks that have to be confronted and overcome. Understanding HOW the auction works has been our key to minimizing our losses.

EVERY STATE IS DIFFERENT

Every U.S. state has the complete latitude to determine how properties are titled and owned and the process for foreclosure. There is NOT a national process for deeding properties. It is divided up state by state. So, for example, if you would like to buy properties at the Los Angeles, CA foreclosure auction like I have, you FIRST need to understand California foreclosure law. Then you need to find out locally when and how often the auction is held. Next, you need to understand everything from how to buy the properties (having cashier's checks on deposit) to what the local protocol is for bidding and if there is a redemption period for the properties after you purchase them.

TRUST DEED VS. MORTGAGE

One of the biggest differences from state to state is the way the property is deeded. States are either classed as trust deed states or mortgage states. These are also sometimes called non-judicial (trust deed) and judicial (mortgage). Basically this means that with a judicial foreclosure, you have to take the borrower to court and get a judgment from the judge to take the house back. This is also why most foreclosure auctions take place at the local courthouse or on the courthouse steps.

The Mortgage-only states are as follows: Alabama, Connecticut, Delaware, Florida, Indiana, Iowa, Kansas, Louisiana, New Jersey, New York, North Dakota, Ohio, Oklahoma, Pennsylvania, South Carolina, Vermont, and Wisconsin.

All other states are considered Deed of Trust states. Both documents place a lien on the house which allows the lender to sell the property if the borrower can't meet the terms. The big difference is that with a deed of trust, the lender does NOT have to go through a lengthy court proceeding to foreclose and take the property back.

A Deed of Trust allows a loan to be secured for a property with the involvement of a third party called a trustee. The trustee is usually a lawyer, escrow company, or title insurance company. A foreclosure involving a deed of trust can usually be completed within a couple of months from the time the borrower gets behind 90 days on their mortgage.

REDEMPTION

The one thing to keep in mind with Trust Deeds is many have a redemption period. This just means, for example, if you were to buy a house for $100,000 that is worth $200,000, if the homeowner comes up with $100,000 in the redemption period, they can buy the house back from you. So if you have started fixing it up, you would be completely out of luck and you would lose any additional money you put into the deal. States with redemption periods are as follows:

- Alabama - 12 months

- Colorado - 75 days
- Indiana - 3 months
- Iowa – 6 months
- Kansas – 6-12 months
- Michigan – 6 months
- Minnesota – 6 months
- New Jersey – 10 days
- North Dakota – 60 days
- Wyoming – 3 months

If you do make the decision to buy foreclosure properties with a redemption period, you want to make sure you don't spend too much money on the house until you get the deed and THEN get title insurance.

STEPS TO TAKING ACTION

1. Start with one state and one specific market and work within that state. Every market has its own set of written and unwritten rules. If you try to work more than one market at a time, you are setting yourself up for huge volatility in your results.
2. Once you have picked a market, make sure you spend time getting to know it INTIMATELY! You shouldn't attempt to buy at foreclosure auction until you can

      i.   Estimate construction on a house by looking at the exterior

     ii.   Have rent rates memorized street by street

   iii.   Have after repair values memorized street by street

   iv.   Have a need for more than 5 properties a month (in my opinion this is critical in order to make sure when you get bad deals they don't hurt you as badly)

     v.   Have at least $250,000 liquid

3. After market knowledge, you need to figure out all of the state foreclosure laws. Almost every state has digital access easily found with a web search. It is critical you understand the nuances of HOW a property is foreclosed in order to understand HOW the auction works and WHAT your risks are.

4. Finally, I strongly recommend you attend at least 3 auctions before you actually attempt to purchase. Get to know who the local players are, find out where they are buying properties, what prices they are paying, and see if you can understand any of the unwritten customs every market develops.

SUMMARY

To my knowledge, there is no comprehensive summary of how to buy foreclosure properties in every market in the

US. Hopefully from reading this chapter, you have clarity on how to move forward learning an individual market and understand steps to take in order to pull the trigger and bid on deals. I can think of few things as exciting as getting an "A+" deal. Just remember that some of the worst "F" deals I've seen other investors purchase came from not doing their homework, not understanding what they were buying, and not really knowing the market intimately like they should.

Chapter Twelve – FLIPPING PROPERTIES TO HOMEOWNERS

Countless books, TV shows, weekend seminars, and group discussions have been dedicated to the topic of flipping properties. By no means do I intend to comprehensively cover this topic. However, through the thousands of properties I have purchased, fixed and flipped, there are some nuggets of valuable advice as well as formulas I use over and over to make sure I'm getting a good deal and hitting my targeted profits. So consider this chapter as something you can refer to down the road once you have completed a few flips. If you have already been in the game and done some deals, then you will know how "true" and valuable these pointers can be.

Let me start by digging into the most COMMON mistakes other investors make when trying to flip properties.

I. *You make money when you BUY:* Fledgling investors will show me detailed spreadsheets illustrating how much profit they will make BECAUSE they are borrowing money and the rate of return on their cash goes up (completely forgetting they are taking on more RISK to offset that return). Or they will show me how they conservatively estimated the repair work, and they're just SURE they can get it done for cheaper (thereby driving up the return). Finally and possibly worst, is they will show how the appreciation will drag the value up on the property by the time they have rehabbed it. While these are all good things which happen to improve cash on cash return, NOTHING can replace getting the property for pennies on the dollar. Instead, buy it for fifty cents on the dollar. After repairs, financing, and closing costs, you'll be no more than seventy cents on the dollar into the deal.

II.   *Construction Decisions and Pricing:*

I have flipped millions of dollars' worth of properties since 2000. I have broker's licenses in multiple states. I own construction companies and have real estate agents working for me. What I never take on myself - decisions on construction finishes and listing price. I have learned to rely on my power team of experts: architects, expert LOCAL market realtors, and contractors with experience rehabbing residential flips. Trying to figure out whether to put white pine flooring or bamboo or if the house should be listed for $109k versus $119k, I leave for my staff whose EXPERIENCE in that area will give the best results.

III. *Screw up ARV and forget costs:* Deciding on a listing price for a property is like forecasting the weather: it's an educated guess. ARV changes like the wind and should ONLY be decided by an agent who has SPECIFIC neighborhood knowledge. I prefer agents who live in the area where you are listing the home, who do flips themselves in that area (sometimes I meet them at auction competing with me to bid on homes), OR who have more than 30% of the listings in that area. Someone who can give property by property details happening in that area over the past six months is vital to me. If they don't know their market THAT well, then I worry about leaving money on the table or listing a property too high.

As far as costs and expenses, many rookie investors focus on the GROSS profits on the deal and forget commissions, closing costs, pro-rated taxes, repairs resulting from home inspections, construction insurance, utilities, attorney fees, and title and escrow fees. In my experience, these fees average 10% of the sales price of a deal. That is a lot of money if you are only calculating 15% gross profits!

IV. *Choose the wrong neighborhood to begin with:* I always joke that everyone wants to invest in "sexy" deals and show their friends the "sexy" properties they own. Think about the reaction from telling other investors you are a "commercial developer" vs. a "mobile home park owner." There is a mental hierarchy in the type of investing many investors think they want to do. When it comes to flipping, most investors want to flip houses in the same type of neighborhood where they live or WANT to live when purchasing their next house.

If you were to take the town you live in, and map out all of the homes that have been listed and sold for the past 18 months, then go drive those areas, you would be shocked at where the highest concentration of activity is taking place. No matter where you go in the US, the highest percentage of homes bought and sold tend to be in the blue collar neighborhoods. These are the neighborhoods where people are graduating from renter to starter home or from starter home to second home. Generally these would NOT be considered "sexy" areas. One house flipper I know considers her properties "works of art", allowing her ego to be wrapped up in the deals which results in her putting too much money put into the rehab. In fact, she really ends up splitting the profits with her contractor.

Lastly, remember it is MUCH harder doing flips for higher-end clientele. They are picky about everything, and I don't like to guess likes and dislikes. Entry level buyers are simply happy with granite in the kitchen, and don't mind the color (well at least not as much as a higher end client would!)

FORMULA – calculating the deal

A couple of months ago, an investor asked if she could have all the formulas I use to calculate deals. I laughed and responded that I wish it was that neat and tidy, I would have created a smartphone app long ago to spit out numbers and made a fortune from it! BEWARE of any company or app telling you they have some special calculator or software that tells what to pay for deals or where to find the best deals. In my opinion, I have not seen ANY software, app, or website that will replace specialized knowledge of the following items:

- *After Repair Values*
- *Construction Amount*
- *Rent Rates*

- *Current Market Value*

- *Expenses*

Everything I have seen breaks down with the assumptions that have to be made in order to get a value or profit amount or sales price. By the time you have entered in all the assumptions there are so many "guesses" that the results you come up with become useless.

Here is the way I evaluate a flip:

FLIPPING FORMULA

- PURCHASE PRICE $25K
- REHAB $50K
- ALL IN $75K
- I WILL NOT FLIP THIS HOUSE UNLESS I CAN NET 25%
- 25% OF $75K = $18,750
- IF I CAN'T SELL THIS HOUSE FOR $103K OR MORE THEN I WILL WHOLESALE IT
- DON'T FORGET YOU PAY ABOUT 10% ON THE BACK END – CLOSING COSTS, COMMISSIONS, REPAIRS REQUESTED BY THE BUYER

As you can see, it is a simple formula, all based around the TARGET RETURN ON INVESTMENT. When doing a flip, I must make at LEAST 25% or I won't move forward on that deal. We completed a deal in Dallas TX, and when we ran the numbers initially, I thought I would make 30%. However we miscalculated the ARV and had to drop the price – TWICE; then, when we finally got a buyer, the inspector found an issue with the hot water heater and several other items costing me several thousand dollars. In addition, some vandalism occurred which was another cost to me. When all was said and done, I only made 19% on the deal.

Looking at cash on cash return only is a mistake. So they will say, "Look I only put $10,000 down with my Hard Money Lender and made $10k in profit so my return on investment was 100%. What a great deal!" I personally don't like running the numbers this way. Assume you are doing the deal with ALL CASH. What will your net return be after you sell the house? If it's 25% then it's a good deal. I will hear other investors say, "But Aaron, that just isn't realistic in San Francisco, or Miami etc.." My answer is, "Then you shouldn't be rehabbing and listing those deals. Just mark them up 5 or 10K and sell them to some other sucker dumb enough to do a flip on tight margins less than 25%."

One of my best secrets for making money in a hyper market like Denver or Phoenix or California is to flip mobile homes. Yes, single wide, double wide, manufactured homes sitting in RV and mobile home parks!! More and more Boomers are looking to downsize, and many first generation immigrant workers are looking to graduate from renting to owning. I am constantly encouraging my clients and partners from these hyper-markets to educate themselves on mobile homes and mobile home parks and begin flipping there.

One final thought: *"EVERY PROPERTY IS A FLIP <u>AND</u> EVERY PROPERTY IS A HOLD."* It's naive to try to classify a property as one or the other. Consider you have a property you call a "HOLD" or a "RENTAL." But don't you need insurance for both "FLIPS" and "HOLDS"?? Don't you need a good tax strategy? Don't you need to hold properties in an entity like an LLC or S CORP? Don't you need title and escrow ultimately? Whether you hold it for three months or 300 months, isn't it really the same difference? I've had properties I thought I would flip in a couple months, but took twelve months before I could sell them. If I purchase a property and rent it for 120 months and then sell it, wasn't that just a 10 year flip? My point is there is a blurred line between flips and holds, and when investors ask me which I like better, I always say, "I like to sell properties when I can maximize my profits and minimize my tax liability." Savvy investors learn to look at many variables, weigh them out, and distill them down to action plans. There is always uncertainty and an element of gambling that goes into that decision. But following your gut after you've consulted with your power team is how you make money and move forward.

Chapter Thirteen - ACTIVE VS. PASSIVE. HIGH VALUE VS LOW VALUE

5,6,7,8 & 9 figure mindset

Several years ago, a friend of mine said to me, "Aaron, I bet that only 2% of the time you spend "working" each day actually makes you money. I bet the rest of your day is filled with *minutia* – things you need to do but don't make you money – and if you could increase your "working" day to be just 10% of money-making-activities, you will double or even triple your income."

When he challenged me with this thought, I laughed. Then I couldn't get it out of my mind. I started dividing my daily activities into two categories: that which made me money and that which were minutia. To my horror I realized how right he was. For instance, paying contractors, something that needs to be done, didn't MAKE me money. I started to make a list of the things that I did that actually made me money each day:

Taking calls from leads on my marketing
Driving properties
Talking to sellers and prospective tenants
Writing up offers and negotiating new deals
Raising money from partners for new deals
Learning about new marketing techniques to grow my business (like Google adwords)

Then I started a list of all the things I do each day that DON'T make me money directly I stopped after 40! My friend, who has an "8 figure" income, challenged me and identified a huge blind spot in my daily work efforts. I like to say that this friend has an "8-figure" mindset and I know for a fact his net worth is over 8 figures and I personally watched him make an 8 figure income one year. As we worked together, I realized there were many things he, with an 8 figure mindset, focused on, said to himself, obsessed about, and incorporated into everything he did.

When I started my real estate investing journey, I made a $40,000/year salary. This 5 figure income CERTAINLY came with a 5 figure mindset about money. For example, I would get excited about getting a tax refund check each year. This was like getting a bonus. I never thought about the fact that

A. I was just getting back my own money

B. I had essentially loaned it to the Federal and State government for a year

C. I wasn't being paid any interest on this loan

Sounds embarrassing, huh? 5-figure mindset investors can never become 6-figure mindset investors till they learn: 6-

figure work ethic, 6-figure fiscal discipline and 6-figure vision. HOWEVER, 7 and 8 figure net worth investors know that to EARN a 7 or 8 figure income is virtually impossible. You can only INVEST your way to 7 or 8 figure net worth…. The three most common ways to invest are real estate, start a business, and securities. When you INVEST your way to a 7, 8 or 9 figure income/net worth it actually changes the QUALITY of your life. You have free time to build your life doing the things you WANT to do vs HAVE to do. These are the important "truths" I have learned over the years that have helped me graduate from a 5-figure mindset to and 8-figure mindset. I currently am mastering the truths and principals about investing money seen in 9-figure mindset individuals and it's exciting to say the least. Once you internalize the idea, simply mastering KNOWLEDGE and then acting upon it is all you need to do to be successful it will change the way you go about all of your efforts.

High Value and Low Value Activities

For years, I have traveled around the country almost every month meeting with new investors. Frequently, I buy lunch for several hundred investors and teach them about our turnkey business model for investing. I also try to teach some of the important things I've learned about money. A couple years ago, I was in Seattle doing a luncheon and a Microsoft employee named Mike came up to me and wanted to talk to me afterwards. He said, "Aaron I really liked what you said today about minutia. It was funny because I found myself wondering if you had ever worked for Microsoft." I laughed and said, "I can guarantee you that isn't the case." He said, "Well you know, your speech about minutia and eliminating it from your life is a concept they teach and is at the core of how they run their company." I was surprised and kind of giddy at the same time. Look at this excerpt from Microsoft 2013 Annual Shareholder letter:

> *"As we go to market, we will primarily monetize our high-value activities by leading with devices and enterprise services. In this model, our consumer services such as Bing and Skype will differentiate our devices and serve as an on-ramp to our enterprise services while generating some revenue from subscriptions and advertising."*

Mike went on to explain that every employee at Microsoft is asked to look at their time each day and hold it up to the criteria of "high-value" and "low-value" activities. So for example, if you are a computer programmer at Microsoft, cleaning the bathroom would be a low value activity. HOWEVER, if you are a custodian at Microsoft, then cleaning the toilet is a "high-value" activity.

I have seen countless examples of 7, 8 and 9-figure net worth individuals who have learned to separate out high value and low value activities in their daily lives and spend the MAJORITY of their time working on high value activities.

Have you used the phrase, "I don't have enough time" in the past year? For many of you, this is the excuse you use for not educating yourself financially, or starting a business or investing in real estate. I can't tell you enough what an insidious 5-figure mindset belief this is. I would contend if you simply track how you spend your time and filter it between high value and low value and eliminate low value activity time wasters that don't make you any money, you

DO have the time to invest, you DO have the time to educate yourself, and you DO have the time to move your financial future forward.

Let's look at landscaping. How many hours have you potentially wasted in the last year cutting your grass, weeding your garden, planting flowers, raking leaves, etc. What if you paid someone to do that for you (because it's a low value activity in terms of MAKING money (not talking about if it's your hobby) and instead focused that time on one high value activity for making money. Like wholesaling properties. Finding just ONE deal per year could pay for 10 years of landscaping. 5 figure mindset investors say, "I can't afford a landscaper, housekeeper, chef, personal assistant." 7 figure mindset investors say, "I can't afford to spend my time on those low value activities because my time is the ONE resource I have a limited amount of each day."

Active v. passive

In 2012 the Super Bowl came to Indianapolis. My friend Dave and his dad owned a bar downtown just blocks from the stadium. They KNEW during the month the Super Bowl was held, they were going to break ALL sales records at the bar. About 9 months before the Super Bowl, Dave, his dad, and I sat down to discuss a proposal they had for me to loan them money for the bar.

Dave and his Dad wanted to purchase a liquor license that would allow them to sell hard liquor in addition to the beer and wine they were already allowed to sell (going from a 2 way liquor license to a 3 way liquor license). They also wanted to add some cosmetic improvements to the bar. They were interested in borrowing $75,000 from me.

I was hesitant to loan money to a business without a lot of physical assets to secure my money. I also smelled an opportunity. I proposed to Dave and his dad that instead of an unsecured loan, I was MORE interested in having a 20% ownership in the bar that they could buy me out of at any time. I wanted to take on MORE risk, but not risk losing all of my $75k if the bar ultimately failed. But the flip side would be that I would MAKE much more in profit than I ever would as a creditor.

After negotiating back and forth for a few weeks, David and his dad agreed to make me a partner in be able to eat at the bar and be treated like everyone else. I wanted all of the transparency and upside of ownership but NONE of the headaches. Dave and his dad actually LOVED this idea because they had been concerned I would come in and want to run the show. It was actually just the opposite. I wanted there to be only one boss (Dave) whom I would hold accountable for his management abilities and ultimately RESULTS as a decision maker. What I really wanted was a COMPLETELY passive investment.

I have seen 7, 8 and 9 figure mentality investors are OBSESSED with passive investments. They see their active investments as something that generates income FOR their passive investments and to create new passive investments. You have the same 24 hours in a day I have. ACTIVE investments take some of that time. PASSIVE investments should take no more than 1/10th of that time. My $75,000 investment in Dave's bar almost doubled over the next couple of years. I made almost 30% return a year on my investment. I didn't spend one minute pouring drinks, washing dishes, kicking out drunk patrons, working nights and weekends, unloading beer kegs, filling in for sick employees or anything of that ACTIVE nature. In fact, I had the best seat in the house whenever I stopped by and Dave was there. All the employees knew me as Dave's friend.

When I transitioned from high school teacher to full time investor, I thought my vision was to

- *Buy 10 new houses to flip every month*
- *Have 10 houses on the market to sell at the same time*
- *Be working on 10 houses to get ready to flip*

To my horror, I found when I got close to achieving those goals, I had simply traded my rewarding and fulfilling career as a teacher for a stressful and mind numbing JOB as an ACTIVE income house flipper. I was making ten times more money but working five times more and my life wasn't getting any better.

The only way you will create more time for yourself and truly **fire your boss** is to embrace passive investments. I find many people understand rental properties as a great passive investment, so they buy a few and manage the properties themselves!! Managing your own rental properties is STILL active income, and most people are now doing property management on their own properties for $15/hour (that is what I pay a property manager starting out). I have one dentist friend who works in his dental practice Monday through Thursday and then when his practice is closed on Fridays, he does handyman work on his properties and collects rents from his tenants. I was teasing him about how dumb this was and I said, "Let's walk through the math. You work 10 hours a day, 4 days a week for 45 weeks a year as a dentist. That's 180 days a year. You make $600,000 a year - so based on 1800 hours fixing teeth, your hourly time is worth $333 hour. Since you spend 5 hours on 45 Fridays as a property manager doing $15/hour work you are really only saving $3,375 worth of labor. You would only have to work ONE EXTRA DAY at your dental practice a year and pay someone to manage your properties and you could take the other 44 Fridays and go do something fun!"

He said, "When you put it like that Aaron, I sound like an idiot for managing my own properties!" I laughed and said, "Your words, not mine; but you should really think about what your time is WORTH and if you are spending at least 80% of your active income time on high value activities."

I know I have introduced a lot of new ideas in this chapter, but let me simplify into one sentence something you could put on a yellow sticky note in your bathroom…

7 figure net worth individuals

focus on active income to invest

in passive investments while

dividing their day into high value

activities that maximize their

earning power!

Chapter Fourteen - UNDERSTANDING THE

FOUR C'S OF REAL ESTATE INVESTING

I am concerned about how overly concerned investors are with cash flow from their rental properties as the most important benefit, and how little they regard the importance of the other VALUABLE benefits that come from owning cash flow properties.

There are four main benefits stemming from cash flow property ownership.

I will briefly touch on each of these, but the bigger issue is to accurately focus in a way which allows you to put a proper VALUE on the investment in the context of the other investments.

If I asked a 5 or 6 figure mindset investor to put these four things into a pie chart showing each one's relative importance in the big picture, it would most likely look like this:

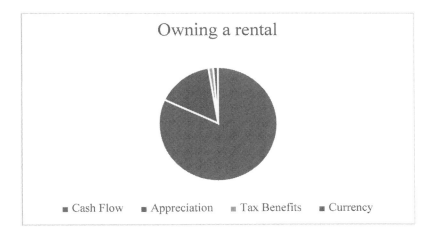

You may have noticed on the first chart outlining the benefits of owning rental properties, I used the phrase "risk mitigation" next to cash flow. I have a friend named Doug who works almost exclusively with big Wall Street funds that buy and own thousands of rental properties. When they talk about cash flow internally, they almost always refer to it as "risk mitigation", meaning, the property wasn't necessarily purchased FOR the cash flow, but it's nice to collect it and it will help offset any surprises from the property like unplanned repairs or expenses.

This pie chart shows a 5 figure mindset investor's view on owning a rental. AATCF… (All About The Cash Flow). Let's take a look at the other benefits

1. *CASH FLOW – RISK MITIGATION*
2. *CAPITAL APPRECIATION & EQUITY*
3. *TAX BENEFITS*
4. *CURRENCY FLUCTUATIONS*

one by one to in order to understand they are each equally as important.

Capital Appreciation & Equity

To me, these are equally as important as the few hundred bucks I get every month from the properties I own. Generally, I can count on $300-500 a month in net income (after paying taxes, management, insurance, and escrowing for repairs and vacancy) for each house that I own. Imagine what owning ten of these properties would do for your financial life? $3000-$5000 a month – a sort of pension – flowing in each month to save for retirement. It's a beautiful thing to be sure! HOWEVER, what if on each house you had $30,000 in equity... or $50,000 per property and they were going up 5% a year in value? Instead of owning a pension which cuts you a check every month and for which you have to pay taxes on, you now own a pension with a piggy bank component you can utilize if you have big ticket item expenditures come up. I have one client who took his properties, went to a local bank, and set up a line of equity on his houses. He lives in complete peace financially; if he has some financial catastrophe pop up, he knows he will be able to write a check. I call these tragedies C.L.E.'s (Catastrophic Life Event). Examples of these would be:

Cancer

Death of a spouse

Loss of Job

Death of a child

Natural disaster

Divorce

We never know when a C.L.E. will arise, but we always know they will. Having the ability to sell a house and use the equity to cover expenses is something a pension, or an annuity, could never accomplish.

I have met FEW investors who have made a double digit return on their 401K or IRA invested in the stock market over a 10 year period. I currently manage THOUSANDS of properties for myself and others that easily make 5% appreciation per year, and 5% from the rents. It is not difficult to accomplish double digit growth to your net

worth by passively owning rental properties. In fact, in my

next chapter you will learn the four criteria I have

developed over time of the qualities a great rental market

should have.

A couple of years ago I was conducting a monthly Meetup

group in Dallas with my partners there. I spoke about

investing for about an hour when a gentleman came up to

me and said, "You know Aaron, you shouldn't really try

and quantify equity or appreciation as part of your

evaluation of your properties. The old rule of thumb is that

equity isn't "real" until you sell the property". I replied,

"That's interesting, because almost every REIT that I have

worked with, or private equity fund I know that owns rental

properties, quantifies these amounts in their quarterly and

annual communications. Sure you don't have the money in

your pocket like you do with rents, but that doesn't mean you haven't EARNED the returns." I wanted to tell him he was viewing investing from a 6 figure mindset standpoint, but I figured it would only offend him and I didn't have time to explain anyway☺. However, equity and appreciation are real factors confirming you made a good financial decision to buy and continuing to hold the property and rent it is a good decision going forward. I have a property I bought in Indianapolis that has appreciated 300% in 10 years' time. Just because I haven't sold it yet, DOESN'T mean I haven't made those returns or that I DON'T have a ton of equity. I just haven't put the cash in my pocket yet. Sure, there will be volatility and it could go up and down over time, but that's something ALL investments do. There is no guarantee - which is why we call it investing!

Tax Benefits

What tax bracket are you in? How much did you pay in taxes last year? What was the exact rate you paid? I find few W2 investors who can answer this question. Investors think of taxes as a necessary evil, something they focus on in April when they swing by Walmart and pick up Turbo Tax. I

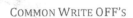

COMMON WRITE OFF'S
- INTEREST
- REPAIRS
- DEPRECIATION
- TRAVEL
- VEHICLES
- HOME OFFICE
- EMPLOYEES
- LOSSES
- INSURANCE
- LEGAL AND PROFESSIONS

know this because when I was teaching high school I had NO CLUE how to answer these questions. Did you know that in 2011 on $13.7 million dollars in earned income, Mitt Romney only paid 14.1% tax rate? That means he wrote out a check to IRS for approx. $1.9M. However, based on

that income, he SHOULD have been in the 35% tax bracket

and should have written out a check for $4.795M to the

IRS. HOW IS THIS POSSIBLE? Our tax code has a lot of

preferences for investment income over labor (active)

income. Mitt Romney pays people to take advantage of

every single one!

Imagine a scenario where you have two individuals who

made $1M last year. One was a lawyer whose firm paid

him $1M and one was a real estate investor who took

advantages of these tax benefits. The lawyer has very few

deductions (write offs) and pays 40% tax rate so the state

and federal governments receive $400k of his money.

Meanwhile, the real estate investor works with CPAs and

other professionals to carefully plan his repairs and

improvements as well as other expenses and he only has to

write checks to the IRS for $150,000 at the end of the year.
5 and 6 figure mindset investors tend NOT to think of tax
benefits as REAL benefits from passively owning rental
properties. This is MADNESS because paying less money
to the IRS is REAL MONEY you keep at the end of the
year. I can only think this is because of their current
ignorance of how much they give up in income tax
currently and, unfortunately, they can't see a rental
property as reducing their rate.

Every 7, 8, & 9 figure mindset individual I have ever met
spends time and money planning out their expenditures and
tax strategy – just like Mr. Romney. Now imagine a rental
property which makes you 5% appreciation, 5% cash flow,
and 2% tax benefits a year. That's 12% increase on your
net worth and money you have. Did you make 12% on
your money last year? Passively? Are you starting to

understand how wealthy people THINK and PLAN differently from you? It was a huge "smack in the forehead" to me as I started to understand these concepts AND incorporate them into everything I do. Being wealthy is a mindset. First you have to learn the principles and then incorporate them into everything you do.

Currency Fluctuations

This is the one year currency fluctuation between the US dollar and the Singapore Dollar:

(http://www.xe.com/currencycharts/?from=USD&to=SGD)

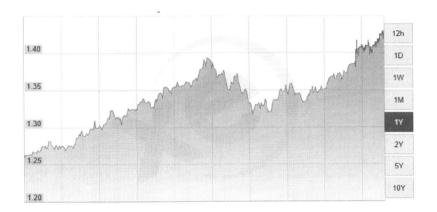

Twelve months ago, I had a client from Singapore purchase a property located in Indianapolis. I sold it to the client for $60,000 USD.

At the time $1 USD = $1.26 Singapore dollars. So the cost of the property for my investor was $75,000 of his Singapore Dollars. As you can see from the chart, the US dollar has further strengthened against the Singapore dollar from Sept 2014 to Sept 2015. If that same investor wanted to buy another property from me today, he would have to convert $84,720 Singapore dollars to get the same $60,000.

One year ago when I sold him the property, it rented for $700/month. Every month I was sending him $882 Singapore dollars. The property is still rented for $700/month (USD) yet now I send him $987 Singapore dollars a month. He has had a 12% increase in rent JUST because of currency fluctuations. I have had investors who have asked me to HOLD their rent in my escrow account JUST because the money is trending a certain way and every day the dollar strengthens or weakens is an opportunity to make money.

Can you see once again how the factors outside of just rental income become a HUGE part of the overall investment? I have clients from all around the world who have made 5% from the rents, 5% from the appreciation,

2% in tax benefits and 5-10% just from currency fluctuations in the past year - 15-25% PASSIVE returns from owning rentals in the US.

Here's what the pie chart would look like in the mind of a 7, 8 or 9 figure mindset investor

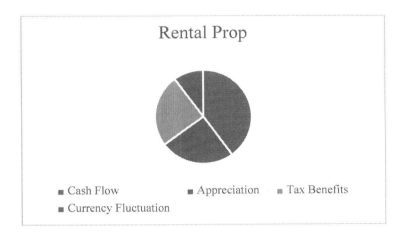

Rental Prop

- Cash Flow
- Appreciation
- Tax Benefits
- Currency Fluctuation

Understanding WHAT you own and if it's a "good investment" is 90% of the battle. Until you learn to evaluate a deal, you won't even recognize great opportunities right in front of your face.

Chapter Fifteen - FOUR FACTORS THAT MAKE

A GREAT MARKET

I constantly get the following questions from investors:

- Why Indianapolis? Why not somewhere I would like to actually visit like Vegas! Why Kansas City, or Charlotte, or Dallas for that matter?

- How do I know where to find the right place or area to buy rentals? Would my own town work?

- What factors do you look at when deciding if you should go into a new market? Do you track any economic metrics that sway your decision?

- What markets are you currently looking at? Where do you think will be a great place to invest in the next 5 or 10 years?

Over fifteen years and thousands of properties later, I have developed 4 main criteria to decide how quickly I sell a property. Sooner or later every property is a flip. It could be 3 months or it could be 300 months. Sometimes you never know.

In 2011 (at the absolute BOTTOM of the last real estate crash), my partners and I went into Las Vegas and bought a ton of properties. Many of these were deals that had sold for $300k+ prior to the 2007 crash of the market. By 2011 they could be purchased for $40-75K. Rents hadn't declined proportionally to property values so it made a ton of sense for us to acquire as many of these as we could. Many of these rented for $900-$1500/month. So just from cash flow we were making 9-15%

Originally we were thinking these would be great rentals. However, by 2012 several big Wall Street funds had the same ideas about Las Vegas as well as many investors all over the US. We were able to sell these deals for 15-50% more than what we paid for them. Our strategy with these homes seemed to change monthly. By 2015 many of these same properties have come back to almost 2006 pricing and higher!

1% Rule of rentals

Before we made the decision to buy those Vegas properties, we used our quick calculation or, what I call, the 1% rule. It's a rule I have used-since my early investing days. If my monthly rent could be 1% or greater than my "all in" number (purchase price + rehab), then I could make enough cash flow in case I couldn't sell it immediately, but I could also always cover my costs and make enough cash flow to hold it until I COULD sell it.

For example:

Purchase a home for $75,000 + Repairs $25,000 = All In $100,000. If I can't get monthly rent of 1% of $100,000 ($1000/mo) then I don't think it will be a great rental property.

I use this formula as a pre-screen before applying my Four Factors that Make a Great Market. If you can't find the 1% rule without going into low income/high crime/low home ownership (ghetto), then find another market in which to buy.

Cheap Houses

Of course "cheap" is completely relative. I usually want to see the ability to buy a home for 50% of the median home price. Obviously in a distressed condition needing significant repairs, but you can't even get these types of properties in markets like San Francisco, South Beach, Manhattan, San Diego or Chicago. This instantly eliminates them from consideration as good rental markets.

4 CRITERIA

1. CHEAP HOUSES
2. LONG TERM STEADY POPULATION GROWTH
3. LOWER THAN AVERAGE UNEMPLOYMENT
4. BUSINESS FRIENDLY STATE GOVERNMENT

One of the main reasons markets run out of cheap houses is because they have a geographic constraint limiting new construction and growth. An ocean, an island, the Mississippi River, a Great Lake, Mountains… the list goes on and on. Markets with "cheap" houses usually have the ability to grow with the population.

Indianapolis, Kansas City, Dallas and Charlotte all share the ability to grow with the population. As a result, there are opportunities to find excellent deals on cheap houses. Houses can be purchased at foreclosure auctions, tax sales, City/County surplus sales, in big portfolios from banks and from private wholesalers. I don't care WHERE the deal comes from, as long as I can buy it cheap, THEN I create value by fixing it up and renting it.

Long Term Steady Population Growth

County	2000	2013	Population Change	Percent Population Change
Hamilton County	182,740	279,315	+96,575	+53%
Hendricks County	104,093	146,759	+42,666	+41%
Hancock County	55,391	69,767	+14,376	+26%
Boone County	46,107	57,275	+11,168	+24%
Johnson County	115,209	140,426	+25,217	+22%
Marion County	860,454	898,448	+37,994	+4%
Putnam County	36,019	37,463	+1,444	+4%
Morgan County	66,689	68,572	+1,883	+3%
Shelby County	43,445	43,906	+461	+1%
Brown County	14,957	15,067	+110	+1%
Madison County	133,358	129,910	-3,448	-3%

Look at this population growth chart from the 11 county Indianapolis, Central Indiana region (http://www.savi.org/population-growth-in-central-indiana/) As you can see, there has been steady long term growth to the area. Many people ask me WHY it's grown like it has, and on one hand I could get into an elaborate discussion of the balance of health care, tourism, sports, and education that comprise this area, but on the other, more simplistic hand I can simply reply, "Who cares!"

If you know a market has been steadily growing for the long term, you don't necessarily have to understand WHY it is growing, because the relocating residents will all need HOUSING. Take a hard look at population growth and the new construction market. Every time there is a discrepancy, or not enough homes being built to keep up with population growth, then it is an opportunity to buy existing homes and convert them to rentals.

One other HUGE factor in this metric is the fact that culturally as a nation, we are at our lowest percentage of homeowners than ever before. Retiring Baby Boomers want to downgrade and/or are forced to sell their home in order to use the equity for their retirement; and 20 and 30 somethings are waiting longer and longer to form households and purchase homes. A simple Google search on this topic will reveal a multitude of studies supporting this trend. There simply has NEVER been a better time to be a landlord than now!

Lower than average unemployment

Indianapolis, Kansas City, Charlotte and Dallas all tend to float 3-5% lower than the national average for unemployment. At the bottom of the market when unemployment reached 9% nationally, these markets were at 7%. As the economy has come back and unemployment has dropped, these markets have dropped as well.

When I was in Singapore last year meeting with investors interested in buying properties in the US, many asked about North Dakota. What did I think of the opportunities there to invest? They pointed out the lowest unemployment rate in the country. (They also cited the explosive population growth.) I was able to give uniquely personal responses because one of my brothers and his partners had actually invested in a trucking company which delivers clean water to the mines and removes fracking water post mining in that area. My brother and his partners are intimately familiar with North Dakota. I'll never forget his comment when asked about the long term viability of North Dakota, "Well, I'm glad we invested in trucks because if oil prices drop, there was nothing there before and there won't be anything there afterwards and we can drive our trucks away." Not two years later, oil did indeed drop and they shut down their operation.

Short term unemployment doesn't impress me. Just like short term population growth isn't anything to get excited about. I would always prefer to see long term steady trends when evaluating a local market for rental property viability. I intend to hold my houses for a long time and even though past performance doesn't guarantee future results, I have found it tends to correlate strongly so I weigh it accordingly.

Business Friendly State Government

As I travel around the world and meet with investors interested in parking their money in US real estate, I find very few understand the differences between state and federal governments. As I describe the different business climates I have experienced, it makes much more sense to choose carefully when purchasing a rental property.

A few examples:

- Evictions in rent control areas vs. business friendly climates. One can take months and thousands of dollars, the other weeks and a few hundred bucks.
- Limited Liability Companies can cost $800/year to maintain in California and $26/year in Indiana.

- Property taxes in Illinois can cost $3000 a year for a $100,000 house and $1000 a year in Indiana for the same $100k house.

- Texas has NO state income tax. You only pay federal taxes on your rental income.

- Judges, courts and the way laws are written can be extremely friendly to investors and others not so much.

The key to remember is until you understand the different ways a state government can help your business, you'll never be dialed into why this is such an important issue. Look for example at this "business friendly" list from the Indiana Economic Development Corporation website listing all the ways Indiana is a good place to do business:

BUSINESS-FRIENDLY

We've methodically created a business environment where conditions are set for success. Whether it's minimizing operating expenses or delivering the workforce training and infrastructure you need to grow, Indiana is one of the most business-friendly states in America.

BEST BUSINESS ENVIRONMENT

- Indiana ranks best in the Midwest and 7th overall in Area Development magazine's Top States for Doing Business survey (Sept. 2014).
- Indiana's business climate ranks best in the Midwest and 5th in the nation in Business Faculties' 2014 State Rankings Report (Aug. 2014).
- Indiana ranks 1st in the Midwest and 7th in the nation as the best place to do business in the Pollina Corporate Top 10 Pro-Business States study (July 2014).
- Indiana ranks 1st in the Midwest and 6th in the nation in Chief Executive magazine's annual Best & Worst States survey (May 2014).

TOP TAX CLIMATE

- Indiana ranks 1st in the Midwest and 8th nationally in the Tax Foundation's 2015 State Business Tax Climate Index (Oct. 2014).

CORPORATE INCOME TAX REDUCTION

Indiana's corporate income tax rate is steadily decreasing from the current 7% to 4.9% by 2021. The tax rate will continue to drop each year as the decrease is phased-in.

A RIGHT-TO-WORK STATE

On February 1, 2012 Indiana became the 23rd state in the nation and the first state in the industrial Midwest to pass right-to-work legislation. This new status creates an even more attractive environment for businesses and entrepreneurs alike to move their operations to the Hoosier State. There is strong evidence that the economy is indeed growing, with companies small and large expanding operations and hiring new workers. With the support of the legislative and executive branches of government, businesses can be encouraged by Indiana's move to join other right-to-work states to better compete for and win America's business.

AAA CREDIT RATING

Indiana is one of only 11 states to earn the top bond rating from all three major credit rating agencies (S&P, Fitch, Moody's).

I believe that all four of my factors must be in place for a market to make sense as a long term hold for rental properties. If you are missing one, then you are simply giving up returns. Many investors are afraid to invest away from where they live (when it comes to real estate), but this is absolutely a 5 figure mindset! As I mentioned in an earlier chapter, if you are truly seeking a passive

investment, you should simply focus on the best market and

then find a team who can help you achieve your goals.

Distance is not an inhibitor in the mind of the 7, 8 and 9

figure investor. Returns are the ONLY focus!

Chapter Sixteen - THE FIVE F's

I meet a lot of unhappy people. Every month I speak to hundreds of investors. It amazes me so many of them think having more money will dramatically change their quality of life. In 2010 I read a study conducted by two researchers from Princeton University – Angus Deaton (an economist) and Daniel Kahneman (a psychologist). Their study won a Nobel Prize for Economics. They polled 450,000 Americans and asked them how they felt the previous day and whether they were living the best possible life for them. They were also asked about their annual income.

Interestingly individuals who make less than $75,000 a year felt more ground down by the by problems, they had.

While those making north of $75,000 a year, individual, temperament, and life circumstances had a bigger impact on their happiness than insolvency. In other words, you have enough to cover a comfortable survival at $75k/year: You can take a vacation, afford a second car, save some money. You aren't concerned about not eating.

This study blew me away. It reinforced what I had personally been finding as an earner whose income had doubled. When I did my first flip I was making $40,000 a year. To get $50,000 profits from one deal changed my life. It instantly doubled my income and created all sorts of new possibilities. However, I found diminishing returns as my income increased. When I doubled my income from $80,000 to $160,000 and then to $320,000 and then to $640,000 I found it wasn't as big of a deal. Sure I took a better vacation, but the better vacation didn't add twice the happiness to my life. Spending a week in Las Vegas versus a week in Monaco, while cool, isn't worth four times the happiness. Driving a $50,000 car versus a $25,000 car is only twice as cool until the new car smell wears off. And wearing a $5000 watch instead of a $400 watch doesn't make me look twelve times as handsome or successful.

I thought a lot about this study. I found over and over again that the people I meet who are the happiest are people whose life has balance. I came up with my list of 'Five F's' used as my own personal "happiness roadmap." Let me give you a few thoughts on each. I have found that when I meet someone unhappy, I am able to trace it back to where they are out of balance in their life. I will use a personal example for each to illustrate why they are meaningful to me. I also have listed them in order of what I think their priority should be in our lives.

Faith

I grew up a member of the LDS church. From my earliest memories, I attended three hours of church every Sunday. When I was in high school, I attended early morning Bible study 180 days a year (matching my school calendar). When I turned nineteen, I applied for and was assigned to serve as a missionary for the LDS church for two years in Venezuela. Though I withdrew my membership from the church years ago and am no longer a member, faith has always been part of my thoughts since my earliest memories.

To me, our "faith" is the collection of values, ideals, ethics, and understanding of god which dictates how we live our life. We make decisions every day about every aspect of our life and filter it through our "Faith." Each person should have a statement which encompasses his faith; for example: *"Faith to me is encompassed by Judeo Christian Values as outlined in the Bible and supported by the values and laws held by the founding fathers and outlined in our Constitution."*

Until you have a personal framework outlining and defining your faith, you run the risk of making decisions in the moment and with emotion. This is a recipe for disaster and will always lead to failure. When teaching high school, I would frequently catch my students trying to cheat on vocabulary quizzes in Spanish class. Their initial reaction at getting caught was embarrassment and sometimes horror of what I would think of them. I used to say, "I'm not offended because I don't think you were trying to cheat me as much as you were simply trying to cheat to help yourself."

I have had employees and partners lie, cheat, and steal. Human nature is that we will make mistakes. Setting an honest framework for what your faith is and how it's defined is critical to help you make decisions you can live with and will contribute to great successes.

Family & Friends

Making money at the expense of family time and friend time is one of the most common balance violations. I have two little boys: nine and eleven. They live in Idaho with their mother. They are my "why" – the reason I have spent hundreds of thousands of dollars and thousands of hours commuting from all over the world to see them every other weekend. We don't value what we haven't sacrificed for, and nothing makes me as happy as being with them and seeing their lives unfold.

If there is one area I have neglected over the years it has been maintaining good friendships. I think many of us have *proximity* friends – people we spend time with because it's easy. They are our neighbors, or our kids play sports together, or we go to the same church. Websites like Facebook have made it even easier to keep up with people from high school. I think the truest friendships are personal connections that exceed what may have initially brought us together (proximity) and have the strength to jump decades of absences and potentially hundreds or thousands of miles of physical distance.

Someone is a true *friend* when I am comfortable with them seeing who I am. We each have different aspects of our personality we trot out for different situations: we have our party-persona, work-persona, mommy/daddy-persona, extended-family-Thanksgiving-persona...the list goes on and on. In my mind, a friend has seen every persona and still wants to be around you, still values you in their lives because you enhance it. I recognize I have a very narrow definition of friendship, but some of the richest and happiest experiences of my life have been an outgrowth of sacrifice for family and stripped down humility with friends. These relationships add the vitality, color, context and story to our narratives making life worth living.

Fitness

430lbs.

That was my father's digital scale reading on the hospital bed when he tragically died at only 57 years of age.

325lbs.

That was the bathroom scale reading in my bathroom at the time of my father's death. I was only 32 years old and had no good excuse for following in his dietary footsteps other than our common love of killing six doughnuts and a quart of milk on Saturday mornings.

255lbs.

My current weight and where my weight has stayed over the past ten years. I'm a big guy at 6'4". So 255 is a 38 waist for me. I'm okay with 255. I would rather be 230, which would be a 36 waist, but I still eat way too much candy for that!!

Just weeks ago I was required to get a physical for another life insurance policy. I was proud my blood pressure was 120/80 and my pulse was 57 bpm! I can't think of the last time I didn't spend 90 minutes, 5 days a week at the gym working out. I have made the commitment to make my health, diet, and weight a conscious focus and priority in my life.

I constantly read articles about obesity being a plague in American culture. We as a nation have never been less healthy, have never had better access to health care, and endless access to understanding the best care of our bodies. If heart disease is the number one killer in our society, then we should be required to have a prescription to supersize our meal at the drive through!!

I have found that in order to find balance in my life when it comes to fitness, I have deliberately structured exercise and healthy food into my daily life. I work out first thing in the morning because otherwise I will find a reason to put it off. I only allow myself two "cheat days" a week to indulge in the pizza, sweets, cheeseburgers, and other trans-fat full food I love. Otherwise I head to the juicing store and buy the kale, broccoli, spinach filled drinks I hate but that make my body feel so great. When I take care of my body, not only am I able to keep a ridiculous work and travel schedule, but I feel fantastic like I'm 42 going on 32. I can honestly say I am healthier now than I was ten years ago. It is a trend I plan to continue. Letting your health and fitness get out of balance is a mistake that has tragic implications.

Finances

When it comes to finances, I have learned several 7 figure mindset truths:

Plugging the sieve of your monthly budget is as important as filling it! A couple of years ago a contractor asked me for a loan because he and his wife had several kids and they needed a second car. I asked him why he needed a loan when he had the money for a second car. He got irritated and insisted he and his wife had gone over their household budget in detail and the $400/mo they needed for a car

143

payment just didn't exist. He told me this as we stood outside my office and while he lit up a cigarette.

I asked him if I could find $600/mo in his budget, would he be willing to name his next child after me? He laughed and said, "Sure! Go for it man." I replied, "Quit smoking. You and your wife each smoke two packs a day at $5 a pack. That's $600/month." He got pretty irritated and said that wasn't fair. They had tried to quit and it was just too hard. I replied that as long as he recognizes in his personal economic value system that cigarettes have a higher value in his life than a second car and possibly even his children, then let's look for something else to cut from the budget. Now he was really mad/offended, "That's not right or fair, you're insinuating that cigarettes are more important than my kids!"

However, it brings up one final truth about finances. If you want to know what your financial values are, make a list of your expenses in order of easiest to hardest to give up. You will be surprised about what you value. So if you spend 100% of your money every month, then a retirement isn't something you care about at all. If that isn't true, then why aren't you putting your money where you think your values are? Mastering these principals is infinitely more important than simply making MORE money or more PASSIVE money. Because with these principles, no amount of money will ever be enough to you.

Fun

Outside of visiting family on holidays, I went years and years without ever taking a vacation. I used this as an entrepreneurial "badge" of sorts that I would hold up to W2s and other business owners to show them how committed I was to my business and its growth. In hindsight this was one of the stupidest things I ever could have done. Fast forward fifteen years later, I try and take a vacation and go somewhere fun every six weeks. It may just be for a day or two, but I have been traveling the world and have learned to embrace everything from a New Year's Eve party in Edinburg, Scotland, to a Mexican cruise with my boys (where I got third place in the hairy chest contest, by the way,) to touring Paris on foot with a GPS and Google translate on my smartphone.

Fun needs to be planned into your life. Fun helps center you and gives you a chance to step back from everything and think of it from a 10,000' perspective. Every year my partners and I take our employees somewhere "fun." We have been to Mexico, we have done Bourbon Street on Halloween, and we have rented a huge cabin and retreated as a group to play games, enjoy great food and each other's company. Admittedly, I have placed fun on the list in terms of priority, but it only takes a couple drops of jalapeno to spice up the whole dish, and you should be incorporating more fun into your life if you truly want balance!

Chapter Seventeen – PPP

In recent speaking engagements, I have frequently joked I would like to write a book titled, *"YOU'RE AN IDIOT IF YOU ARE SAVING FOR YOUR KID'S COLLEGE."* And in small print I want it to say at the bottom of the cover *"(at the expense of your OWN retirement)."*

Think about this concept for a minute, you may have a 529 Plan, or a savings account, or bonds you have been setting aside for your child's education. However, at the same time, you may be woefully underfunding your own retirement. Think for a minute what you need a month to cover your "nut." To me, your "nut" is what you need for your mortgages, bills, food and entertainment. If I were to add everything you've spent over the past year and divide that by twelve, what would THAT number be? $3000/mo? $6500/mo? $10,000/mo?

Now think for a moment what you have put together for your OWN retirement. How much is in your 401k? Are you expecting a pension? How much equity is in your home? Do you have an IRA? If you had to pay off all of your debt and liquidate everything? How much would you have left? What kind of monthly income are you creating for yourself to live off of when you retire? Thousands of investors I have met are on track to replace their monthly income. Even if they assume they'll own their home free and clear and eliminate their mortgage, they are still looking at only having ¼ or ½ of their "nut" in monthly cash flow.

Now that you are thinking about your retirement plans…why would you be setting aside money for your child's education when you are on track to UNDERFUND your own retirement?! You tell yourself you are "helping" your son or daughter with college while avoiding the idea you may outlive your savings. When that happens, you

PPP
- **PRICE OF GAS**
- **TAX REFUND**
- **HOUSEHOLD CHORES**
- **TAKE COME PAY**
- **KIDS COLLEGE FUND**
- **COUPONING**
- **TGIF/2 WEEK VACATION**

will be forced to turn BACK to your children to help you with health care, or living expenses and make yourself a financial burden on them? It's madness!

You're trying to "help" your children but one of the best ways to "help" your children is to NOT be a financial millstone around their neck! I call this type of thinking "PPP" which is short for "poor people's problems." Now I'm in no way trying to make light of low income earners. I'm not ridiculing their situation, or the hard choices they have to make every day. HOWEVER, I noticed when I was "poor", which in my case was when I only earned a 4 figure and 5 figure income, I had numerous financial blind spots. Things like the previous example about college funds for kids were financial hypocrisy or misplaced financial focus and concerns. I would like to give you a few other examples that I thought and believed about money when I was "poor" that changed as I learned to earn and invest my money to arrive at an 8 figure net worth individual today.

Price of Gas

I listen to people all the time discussing gas prices. It hasn't been as bad in 2015 as it was in 2012 when prices were close to $5/gallon. But you could bring this topic up almost anywhere in casual conversation and get lively commiserating about what a burden it is to pay for gasoline on a regular basis.

This is always amusing to me. People complaining about things they can't control. What is most ironic is that many of these same complainers regularly buy food, drinks, and cigarettes in the convenience store at the gas station. Do you realize what the markup on these items is? 100-300%. Think about bottled water at $2 a bottle - that would make the water you buy at the gas station cost $16 a gallon. While you pay $16 a gallon for drinking water (something you can completely control), you complain about the high

price of gasoline (something you have zero control over!!)
This is the epitome of PPP. A tendency to focus and stress
over things that don't and shouldn't matter in the financial
big picture.

Spending Your Tax Return

I remember being SO EXCITED the first time I got a tax
refund check. It was "found money" that I hadn't been
expecting, and I was stoked to spend it. I realized why
local businesses offered refund check specials – applying it
for the down payment on your car or special furniture sales.
I even noticed HR Block get in the game and offer a loan
against your check as soon as they prepared your return (I
always wondered how that was an okay business practice...
seemed fishy to me!)

After I started investing full time in real estate, I went from
a W-2 income earner to a business owner. W-2 is what

salaried employees get paid, and your taxes are withheld from every paycheck. W-2 earners focus on their "take home pay" – the net amount they get every two weeks. After they file for their income taxes, if they have overpaid, then they get the overage back in the form of a refund check. I never stopped to think I was just getting my own money returned to me. To make matters worse, when you get your refund check, there is no interest included in the money you essentially loaned to the federal government. I felt foolish getting excited about getting my money back a year after loaning it to the government and not getting any return on investment.

When you are a business owner you don't focus on "take home pay" – you focus on "adjusted gross income." You pay taxes AFTER the year is complete, not every two weeks. When you calculate your adjusted gross income, you get to deduct business expenses – AKA – write offs!

You then pay taxes on the net income. One of the most

ironic facts about our current system of income taxation is

that the wealthy in this country pay generally the lowest tax

rates. I'll never forget Mitt Romney only having to pay just

above 10% in taxes. I paid a much higher tax rate (twice as

much) as a high school teacher!! You can see why I say

now it's PPP to focus on your take home pay. Because it

means you are giving up the highest percentage of your

income to the government, regardless of how much you

make, when you are a W-2 earner.

Credit score

After reading my first two examples, I am sure you are now

wondering, "How is credit score an example of PPP???"

People with perfect credit are always so proud about their

score. They always announce it with almost a smirk on

their face. Isn't your credit score something you will use your whole life?

Loans can be divided up between two categories: Recourse and Non-Recourse. 100% of the first fifteen loans I ever had – credit card, auto, student loans, home loans, investment home equity loans – were recourse loans. They were tied to my social security number. If I don't pay those loans, then my credit can be ruined, the lender can get a judgment against me, and take back the car or the house or the boat. So the "recourse" isn't just contained to what they loaned you, they can also ruin your credit, and potentially force you into bankruptcy. Initially, I thought ALL loans were recourse loans. It was shocking to me to learn about non-recourse loans. By simply paying a higher interest rate, banks, businesses, and private individuals would all be interested in loaning me money with the only recourse being the hard asset they made against the loan.

Five figure mindset earners generally don't understand money always follows good deals NOT the other way around. IF you have a great company, banks line up to loan you non-recourse loans. If you have a home run deal, then there is an infinite amount of ways to get the money to purchase it, and lenders will be happy to secure their money only with the asset and not your social security/credit score. Now can you see why it's PPP to worry about your credit score? Do you think in 2008 when horrible gambling and decision making almost ruined our economy, the major players in financial services at companies like Lehman Brothers saw a dip in THEIR credit scores? PPP worries about a good credit score. 7

figure mindset worries about getting good deals and then finding the non-recourse money.

Extreme couponing

I mentioned this one earlier – albeit indirectly when I discussed high value and low value activities. I think couponing as a way to save money for the household budget is horribly PPP.

I have a friend Launie, who is one of the BEST real estate brokers I have ever met, and she is also a savvy general contractor who has sold millions of dollars in real estate over the years. She is also a self-described "extreme couponer." She has stories of trips to the store where she walked in with her box of coupons and left with a cart full of "stuff" and not having spent one penny of her own cash. She came to our bus tour in Indianapolis and started laughing when I discussed this topic.

You see, when Launie is working on real estate she easily makes $300/hr from her time and ability. When she works on couponing, she only saves about $50/hr worth of spending at the store. From that standpoint, every time Launie works on coupon tracking, cutting, and organizing she LOSES $250. In her defense, after she listened to my two cents on this topic, she said couponing isn't her obsession but is her hobby, and she never works on it during her 9-5 work day. I need to check in with her and see if she spends as much time on it as she used to!

TGIF/Two weeks of vacation

When in college, I worked at the Showboat Hotel & Casino in Atlantic City, NJ. I was a member of the "Local 54" food servers union. This was a whole different W-2 world that I had never experienced. Phrases like "bidding on schedule", and "priority first out", and employees telling managers they couldn't be made to clean up the glass they just broke because that wasn't part of their negotiated contract and was housekeeping department's duties… were all new and fascinating to me.

The hotel and casino I worked in was open 24/7/365. This created nontraditional schedules for many of the employees. If your days off were Monday and Tuesday, then Wednesday was your "Monday" and Sunday was your "Friday." While amusing to me, this became a constant topic of conversations among workers. Example:

Worker 1: "Today is my Friday and I can't wait to get out of here so my Christmas can begin."

Worker 2: "I hear you! Since Christmas was my Tuesday and I was stuck in this place I am excited to be with my family for a few days and get all of this off my mind."

One variation or another of this exchange happened all the time. You could literally watch people get happier and happier as the end of the day approached, or "Friday" arrived; or the pinnacle – their "two week vacation" time came up. You see, many of these workers made "great money", but had a "horrible career." They didn't have many alternatives where they could make the same kind of money, and they didn't have passion for their work or get excited about new goals and initiatives. Their work life was one of monotony, routine, and focus on anything but the drudgery they had to confront every day.

PPP focuses on these things. PPP devotes its time to "Friday" and two week vacations. 7 figure mindset workers integrate vacation time, work time, and family time into a seamless tapestry of balance (well the good ones do). But what they DON'T obsess over is the end of the work day. They have work goals and passions dictating vacation or when they finish for the day.

If you think my acronym for PPP is coarse or insensitive, then I humbly apologize. I could have inserted "5-figure-mindset" in every example as a politically correct substitute, but I don't think it has the same weight. I am not by any means trivializing poverty or the plight of those less fortunate. I have found when I teach this topic in person, it invariable elicits lively debate and commentary. THAT is my desired result. You must think about the potentially unimportant or misplaced focuses you have had to this point that distract you, and push you away from becoming more financially savvy and maximizing the time you dedicate to work every day.

Chapter Eighteen -KEY POINTS FOR THE INTERNATIONAL INVESTOR

I am not a lawyer. I am not an accountant. I considered filling two pages with just those two sentences to remind you this chapter is to simply outline some key points I have learned from and for my international investors over the years. I am only giving you my two cents on common questions I get and layman answers I provide. The goal of this chapter is not to ADVISE you on tax or legal issues. I am aware that not all information will apply to all investors, but my goal is to bring these issues to light for you so you can go and get personalized advice about each one.

I DO know each of these topics needs your attention as you contemplate investing in the US market and each one needs a specific, and well thought out game plan. When we meet with investors overseas, and whenever possible, I bring trusted lawyers and accountants with me to specifically answer these questions. More than anything, use this chapter as checklist of things to address in order to successfully invest in the US real estate market.

I have been managing properties for investors since 2003. I started managing properties for investors from other countries around 2006. This was a new and limitless market, but one that required a huge learning curve of knowledge. I can tell you my employees always know what time of day it is in Hong Kong, Singapore, Australia, or England. They also know how to use Skype to catch up with clients, as well as the cheapest texting apps, and free Wi-Fi based calls to supplement their emails.

I regularly travel around the world and sell our US properties to investors. I get the same questions over and over and find common misconceptions come from investors regardless of their country of origin. I would like to briefly describe each of these and give you a simplistic summary of the solutions or explanation as a starting point for your education. I envision you taking what I tell you, going to a licensed professional and saying, "I read in Aaron's book that xxxxxxx. Help me understand if this would apply to my situation."

ITIN

Individual taxpayer identification numbers are for federal tax reporting only, and are not intended to serve any other purpose. The IRS issues ITINs to help individuals comply with the U.S. tax laws, and to provide a means to efficiently process and account for tax returns and payments for those not eligible for Social Security Numbers (SSNs).

An ITIN does not authorize work in the U.S. or provide eligibility for Social Security benefits or the Earned Income Tax Credit. It DOES, however, allow the property manager to send you all of your rent without withholding any of it as well as allow a title company to not withhold a portion of your proceeds when you sell a property.

Technically you could apply for an ITIN yourself. I have not personally ever seen one of my clients do this without multiple attempts. I know of accounting firms that can do this for you for around $400 and get it done correctly on the first try. There are a lot of ways you could get this wrong if you do it on your own, so I advise you to use an accountant who has experience applying for them.

TAXES – Federal/State/Property

This is one of the most common areas of confusion I see from international investors. Every person who owns a US rental property needs to file federal and state tax returns and pay local property taxes.

You need an ITIN to file your tax return. I suggest you use a US accountant to file the return. He will need to file a federal return for you and a state return for the state in which your property is located. Your property manager will give him the income and expenses which can be deducted against the rent, and then you will owe the taxes based on the net income. State and federal income taxes are paid once a year.

Local property taxes are usually paid every six months. Most of my investors pay these themselves. You can also wire funds to your accountant, and he can pay them for you. OR if you have a US bank account, you could have a cashier's check issued and paid to the local city or county to whom you owe the taxes.

INSURANCE

If you own a U.S. rental property you should get a landlord insurance policy for it. A good landlord policy will cover your property, but NOT the tenant's possessions. It will cover you for liability if the tenants sue you. If this happens, the insurance company will pay for the lawyer to defend you, and if there is a judgement against you because you lose the court case, then they will pay the settlement (up to $1M in liability coverage is very cheap).

A landlord policy will also cover you in case of fire or tornado, and if you get the correct type of policy, can also cover you from theft, vandalism and even floods or hurricanes.

I prefer working with an Insurance BROKER who has the ability to craft a policy specifically for my needs as an investor. Insurance for a rental property should cost you about $75/month for every $100,000 of property you own. This is a very rough figure but should be a good starting point.

BANK ACCOUNTS

Having a bank account in the U.S. can be a very helpful tool as you scale up your investing. Almost all U.S. banks will require you to appear in person at the bank with your passport in order to open the account. You will want to plan a trip to the US that includes this trip to a local bank.

Once you have the account, your property manager can deposit the rent in it every month for pennies (wiring to your international account can cost $25+ for every wire). You can also issue bill paychecks from the web for maintenance items on your property as well as cashier's checks to the state and federal government for taxes you owe.

I have met investors who mistakenly think having a U.S. bank account will be beneficial for them in getting loans down the road or improve their chances of getting a Visa. To my knowledge, this is not the case. I haven't seen a U.S. bank account do anything BUT help the flow of money.

OWNERSHIP

The U.S. government has no problem with you buying U.S. properties and land in your own name. The government also has no problem with you purchasing U.S. properties using a company or corporation from your own country. Finally, the U.S. government doesn't have a problem with you opening up a U.S. corporation and then using it to purchase property.

Generally, I would advise that you consider using your personal name or a company from your home country to buy your U.S. properties if you are only buying one or two. The costs of setting up a U.S. corporation or entities to buy U.S. properties doesn't justify the expenditure. Now once you get more properties, it will make sense to set up U.S. companies and bank accounts. But I personally wouldn't advise it initially. The costs could wipe out all of your cash flow!

LOANS

To my knowledge, there is no U.S. lender currently offering recourse/low interest loans to international investors. There ARE lenders offering higher interest and shorter term loans to investors. If you want to get leverage to buy your U.S. property, I would recommend an equity line on a property in your home country and use it to buy your US property. This is something I have seen many investors do. The drawback of using nonrecourse lenders is most have a loan term of three to five years. The downside is what you will do when the term expires if you haven't paid the loan balance off.

None of these topics are particularly complicated, or they shouldn't be, if they are evaluated with professional advice. Hopefully you are more aware of them and will incorporate them into your decision making and due diligence process as you move forward on U.S. opportunities.

I have many clients making double digit returns on their U.S. properties. They are seeing five to twelve percent a year from the cash flow, three to twenty percent a year from the capital appreciation, three to ten percent a year from tax benefits and three to ten percent a year from currency fluctuations. To realize these gains, they have set up a personalized plans for each of the six categories mentioned in this chapter. We love our international investors and plan to incorporate our business relationships with them for many years to come.

CONCLUSION

For those of you who read my first book, you may have noticed I have basically doubled the original book with eight additional chapters. I had a proofreader tell me if I could get this book up to 40,000 words, I would really have something special on my hands. I laughed at this because I have always loved brevity in writing. I hate reading someone's book that feels like they had a great idea for a 50 page book but stretched it to 100 pages... to satisfy some perception that a book has to have a certain length to be legitimate.

I personally love that this book can be read in an hour or two. These are my best ideas and truths learned in my first fifteen years of investing. Down the road I intend to add to what I have learned, regardless of the length, in order to teach and convey the ideas and concepts that have helped me the most over the years.

I always say when you lose money while investing, you are paying "tuition" for your education. I have paid millions of dollars in tuition to learn what I have laid out for you here. Hopefully it is a starting point to prevent you from repeating my mistakes and to guide you to greater heights than my 8 figure mindset could ever achieve!